FARTING MAGICAL CREATURES

Magical creatures have farts too.
This is just a fact.

M.T. LOTT
www.facebook.com/authormtlott

Copyright © 2017 by Lake George Press
www.forgottenfairies.com

ISBN-13: 978-1542366106
ISBN-10: 1542366100

FACT: Brownies have terrible gas
— but they like it.

FACT: Unicorn farts smell
like bubble gum.

FACT: Mermaids like to pretend
the ocean is a jacuzzi.

FACT: Sometimes when a dragon
farts, a little fire comes out.

FACT: Leprechauns fart at the other end of the rainbow.

FACT: A Cerberus has
3 times the smell.

FACT: Fairies cause farts.
It's one of their jobs.

FACT: Pegasus really does fart rainbows.

FACT: Gnomes toot every time they bend over. Every time.

FACT: Hippogriffs use their wings to blow the smell away.

FACT: Troll farts are tremendous.

FACT: A trail of bubbles is evidence of the Loch Ness monster.

FACT: Don't scare a Jackalope in the wild. He will fart on you.

FACT: Boy centaurs are gross.

FACT: Technically, a Basilisk farts out of its scent glands.

FACT: Yetis fart snowflakes.

FACT: The baby Chimera's farts are pretty smelly.

FACT: There is nothing that Goblins love more than farting.

FACT: Griffin farts are quite medieval.

FACT: The seals prefer when Selkies pass gas <u>out</u> of the ocean.

FACT: A phoenix has a very fiery blast.

FACT: Will-o'-the-wisps like a nice group toot.

FACT: Sea foam is Hippocamp gas.

FACT: Christmas elves' toots
smell like candy canes.

Connect with M.T. Lott on facebook

www.facebook.com/authormtlott

Coloring books by M.T. Lott

Other books by M.T. Lott

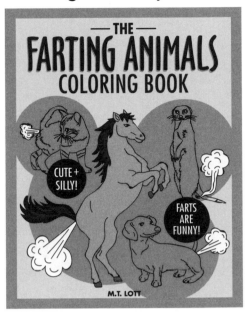

Sample pages from "The Farting Animals Coloring Book"